101 Questions To Ask Before Becoming An Actor

Christopher Strombeck, M.F.A.

TREMOLO
& CREST
PUBLISHING

101 Questions To Ask Before Becoming An Actor

By Christopher Strombeck

Copyright © 2025, Tremolo & Crest Publishing

All rights reserved. No part of this publication may be reproduced, stored in a retrieval system, or transmitted in any form or by any means—electronic, mechanical, photocopying, recording, or otherwise—without the prior written permission of the author, except in the case of brief quotations used in reviews or scholarly articles.

Tremolo & Crest Publishing books may be purchased for educational, business, or sales promotional use.

ISBN: 979-8-9985915-0-1

Contents

Introduction v
101 Questions To Ask Before Becoming An Actor 1
The Last 11 Thoughts 104
Acknowledgments 119
About The Author 121

Introduction

We ask questions about anything and everything to make informed/sound decisions. Without asking the right questions, we could end up in the wrong relationship, attend an inadequate school, or sign a bad contract. Before you jump into acting, there are some key questions you need to answer for yourself. Failing to ask and answer these questions in their entirety could cost you a lot of unnecessary time and money.

Beneath the glamorous surface of red carpets and rave reviews, the entertainment business operates according to its own unique logic. It requires more than just passion; it's about precision, understanding, and strategy. Imagine a Formula 1 driver approaching the famous Monaco circuit for the first time. Do they just accelerate wildly around the corner, hoping for the best? Not at all. They run track simulations, study telemetry data, and analyze every hairpin turn until they can react instinctively. They develop an intimate understanding of the course. The same logic should apply to actors. Before you dive into acting any further, there is a foundational understanding you'll want to build first.

My own foundation was built through many years of trial and error. I spent a lot of time quietly thinking about what this path truly meant, weighing the sacrifices I hadn't expected against the rewards that seemed harder and harder to reach. I had to understand my own motivations and define my artistic integrity step by step. All that searching, along with costly detours and doubts, could have been clearer, easier, or even avoided if a book like this existed. But it didn't. Like many hopeful artists, I was navigating blindly. I believe this lack of guidance is a silent dream killer for many actors. I witnessed talented peers, who had invested everything into their craft—heart, soul, and money—quietly give up before they even had a chance to really get started.

These were not just any actors; they were highly skilled talents, trained at renowned conservatory programs, where they received BFA and MFA degrees. They developed their craft, improved their skills, and dedicated years of their time. But when they faced the realities of the entertainment industry, many realized their dreams were difficult to sustain. Instead of getting stage time or film roles, they often dealt with heavy student debt and struggled to pay their bills. This financial burden has caused many aspiring actors to give up their dreams and find alternative careers.

I saw this happen time and again. A few years after graduating from my conservatory program, classmates I knew who loved theatre and movies started leaving the industry. They weren't just changing jobs or taking breaks; they were quitting acting entirely. Some said they were tired of the constant rejection. Others felt the industry's demands didn't fit the life they wanted. And many couldn't balance their passion with making a living. This is precisely why this book had to be written. Anyone who tells you acting is easy is either lying or delusional. Anyone who binge-watches a hit show and thinks, "I could do that," is missing ninety-nine percent of the iceberg. My purpose here is not to be your cheerleader or your dream-crusher. I'm not here to nudge you towards the spotlight or steer you away from it. My sole aim is to be an honest broker. I am here to arm you with the critical and often uncomfortable questions you must confront before dedicating your time, money, and emotional energy to this demanding path. This isn't about right or wrong choices; it's about making the most informed choice for you, grounded in a clear sense of reality.

The structure of this book is simple. No unnecessary words or technical jargon. It has 101 essential questions for the actor.

Introduction

You'll see a dedicated space below each question for you to fill in your answers, along with an explanation and more details about the question at the bottom of the same page. Be sure to write in your answers for each question. This isn't a book to read once and put away; it's interactive. It's a tool to assist you on your journey, and to act as a touchstone you can return to at any time. This book keeps you connected to your true self and allows you to stay on the path you choose. When you understand who you are, what you believe, and what you truly want, you command respect not only from your peers but also from agents, producers, directors, and everyone you meet.

For some of you, working through these questions might lead to the conclusion that acting isn't your main path, or maybe it's better suited as a fulfilling hobby rather than a full-time career. For others, this book may reinforce your commitment to pursuing acting. My sincere hope is that, whatever your decision, you find this clarity now instead of five years down the line, when the timing isn't right or proper plans haven't been made. This potential heartache and stress can be avoided with a few hours of honest self-reflection and the right questions being asked.

The blunt truth is that acting, as a profession, is not for everyone, just as becoming a brain surgeon or professional poker player isn't for everyone. And that is perfectly okay. If this career were simple, don't you think everyone would be clamoring for it? Who wouldn't want the potential perks of creative fulfillment, accolades, financial rewards, and the chance to impact others? The very allure of that lifestyle underscores its elusiveness. It comes with significant, often unseen, risks. Your personal tolerance for uncertainty, rejection, financial instability, and delayed gratification is a crucial variable you need to assess honestly as you engage with these pages.

And what about those of you who are currently already navigating the acting landscape? Does this book still hold value?

Absolutely. Perhaps even more so. It serves as a vital tool for recalibration, since at this point, you've probably already decided that acting is what you want to do. It prompts you to organize scattered thoughts and to articulate beliefs you might have held instinctively, but haven't examined critically. It forces you to take a stand on your evolving ambitions and goals. Is acting still enriching your life and fueling your spirit? Or has it become a source of chronic stress, a weight pulling you under? As an acting instructor, I learned that everyone has a different path. We cannot, and should not, assume our definitions of success or happiness will map onto everyone else. This book honors your individuality, helping you reconnect with your unique definition of self, no matter what stage you find yourself in.

Again, my mission isn't prescriptive; it's provocative. I aim to equip you with the clarity needed to make decisions that align with your deepest truths. I cannot and will not tell you what decisions to make after you read this book; only you can do that, but you will be equipped to make the decisions that align best with you. The insights in this book will help you discover whether this business is ultimately right for you and provide a new way of thinking. I am genuinely excited for you to embark on this adventure of discovery. So, grab a pen, find a quiet space, and let's begin exploring the 101 questions every individual must ask before deciding to become an actor. Your journey starts now.

Introduction

101 Questions To Ask Before Becoming An Actor

1. Why do you want to become an actor?

Deciding to become an actor is a personal decision often fueled by passion, curiosity, and a desire to explore human nature. Acting enables you to live different lives, see multiple viewpoints, and bring stories to life that can inspire, challenge, and emotionally move audiences. While these are noble goals, some people pursue acting for fame, wealth, or status. It's not about judging right or wrong, but understanding your own motivations. Those seeking fame or money might prioritize the paycheck, while genuine art lovers may be driven by specific characters or stories. Clarifying your reasons helps you stay focused and make choices aligned with your objectives. You may have other reasons or a combination of motives; whatever they are, be as precise as possible in your response.

2. What was that turning point that made you consider acting?

Can you pinpoint a specific moment, experience, or realization that solidified your desire to pursue this career? Maybe it was a dazzling performance that moved you, an acting class that ignited your passion, or the thrill of being on stage or in front of a camera for the first time. Identifying this pivotal moment is important because it serves as a reminder of why you started, helping to keep you motivated during the inevitable challenges of the industry. It also provides a personal story you can share with industry professionals (agents, managers, casting directors), helping them understand your journey and what truly drives you as an actor.

3. What experiences do you have with acting?

Have you taken acting classes, performed in school or community theater, worked on student films, or had any professional on-camera experience? Maybe you've attended workshops, done improv, or even participated in self-produced projects. Whether your experience is extensive or minimal, knowing where you are allows you to set realistic goals, identify areas for growth, and strategically plan your next steps to build your skills and resume.

4. How would you personally rank fame, money, status, character representation, and artistic fulfillment from most important to least important?

Even though some of these aspects may not be reasons for why you want to become an actor, it's undeniable that these factors have a place within the industry (both from the small-scale to large-scale projects). Take a moment to sit back and imagine what it would be like to live out each of these experiences fully and on their own. Which resonates with you the most and delivers a burning desire to achieve? Rank them in order from the most important to the least important.

5. What type of acting (film, TV, theater, voiceover, commercials) interests you most?

Just saying, "I want to become an actor," is too vague. You need to get clear with yourself and define exactly what that means to you. Do you prefer TV, film, commercials, voiceover work, or theater? Although acting is involved in all of these, they do not operate the same way. Film and TV often require a subtlety that closely mimics real life. Commercials typically involve quick shooting sessions and often need a more exaggerated style to sell a product. Voiceover work demands that an actor has total control of their vocal instrument, since physical presence isn't shown. Lastly, theater requires the actor to be aware of the audience as if they are another character in the play. They must be able to hear and see you from the back row. Film acting and its subtleties might not be as effective in this setting. Clarifying which area aligns most with your strengths, interests, and career goals will help you strategically navigate your acting journey.

6. Why acting over any other profession?

Considering the challenges and uncertainty this industry often presents, it's crucial to understand why acting appeals to you more than any other career. Maybe you love telling stories, enjoy the thrill of performing live, or find the creative process deeply rewarding. Whatever it is, honestly identifying what makes acting different for you can help you stay dedicated and focused during tough times or unexpected setbacks in your career. Be very specific and detailed in your response.

7. If you had to do something other than acting, what would it be?

Having a clear understanding of your alternative interests can help you feel more grounded and secure in this unpredictable business. Many see this as a "backup plan" and immediately assign a negative connotation to this, but rather than view it as a bad thing, consider it a safety measure. You wouldn't drive your car without wearing your seatbelt, so why jump into an unpredictable profession without a safety net? A wise man once told me, "Hope for the best, plan for the worst." Having an alternative in case acting doesn't work out not only provides you with a small sense of security, but also marks the start of a plan. The more realistic and interest you have in the alternative, the more secure you will feel.

8. What matters most? Accolades/awards, peer approval, or inner satisfaction? Rank them in order.

To say that we do not enjoy some form of validation or approval for our work would be completely lying to ourselves. If this were true, a bad note in class or a horrendous review would have zero effect on us. Some actors see awards as important milestones that can bring recognition, credibility, and new opportunities. Others may place significantly more value on the respect of their peers or the personal fulfillment that comes from doing meaningful work, regardless of public recognition. These forms of validation play a different role for each of us and carry a very different kind of weight. Understanding how much importance you place on each can help guide the way you measure progress and define success in your career.

9. If you never "make it big," would you still be happy pursuing this career?

Acting, like any other art form, is a highly unpredictable career with many highs and lows. Be completely honest with your answer. Imagine 10 years go by, you audition for many roles, maybe you book something small here and there, maybe you don't, but nobody on the street is asking for your autograph, and no one recognizes you. Would you still be happy pursuing this career? Write in detail for yourself why or why not.

10. Can you handle rejection?

You may face frequent auditions without callbacks, projects falling through, or even receiving criticism of your work. Being consistently turned down can affect your self-esteem, self-worth, confidence, and motivation. It's essential to honestly assess whether you are able to separate professional rejection from personal value. Developing a strong mindset and coping strategies early on can help you navigate rejection more effectively throughout your acting career.

11. Can you handle constructive criticism?

Acting regularly involves feedback from directors, acting coaches, casting directors, and/or fellow actors. Constructive criticism can sometimes feel personal or difficult to accept, especially if you're deeply invested in your work. It's crucial to honestly evaluate whether you are currently mature enough to truly listen, process, and apply feedback without becoming defensive or discouraged. Learning to welcome constructive criticism as a tool for growth can significantly enhance your skills and help you become a stronger, more adaptable actor over time.

12. What does success as an actor look like for you?

Defining your personal vision of success is critical, as it sets clear expectations and helps you measure progress realistically. For some, success might mean fame, awards, or financial stability. For others, it could be steady work in meaningful projects, respect from peers, or simply the satisfaction of continually improving one's craft. Understanding exactly what success means to you will allow you to make informed choices, set achievable goals, and maintain your motivation throughout your acting journey.

13. What are your short-term career goals?

Clearly identifying these goals helps you create practical steps toward your bigger dreams. Short-term goals might include attending regular acting classes, booking your first professional audition, securing representation from an agent or manager, or landing small roles in student or independent projects to build your experience and *reel*. Defining these immediate objectives will not only keep you motivated, but also provide clear direction, structure, and measurable progress as you move forward in your acting career.

14. What are your long-term career goals?

Knowing the answers to this can help you establish a clear vision for your acting career and keep you focused on the bigger picture. Long-term goals might include booking recurring roles, starring in major film/theater productions, gaining representation by top-tier agents/managers, achieving financial stability through acting alone, or branching out into directing and/or producing. Defining these broader objectives creates a roadmap that can guide your career decisions forward, helping you prioritize opportunities and ensuring you're consistently moving in a direction you truly want to go.

15. What genre of movie/TV would you like to do?

Clarifying your preferred genres, whether it's comedy, drama, action, horror, sci-fi, thriller, or romance, allows you to focus your efforts and energy strategically. Comedy requires sharp timing and improvisational skills; drama demands emotional depth and vulnerability; action often involves physical training and stamina; horror might challenge your ability to evoke fear and suspense; sci-fi and fantasy require imagination and adaptability; thriller roles often explore psychological intensity; and romance relies on chemistry and a palpable emotional connection. Knowing your genre preferences helps you pursue suitable projects, tailor your training, and effectively communicate your brand to directors, casting directors, agents, and other industry professionals.

16. What genre of movie/TV would you never do?

It's important to set clear personal boundaries early on in your career, especially regarding roles or genres you're uncomfortable with or feel don't align with your personal values or image. For example, some actors might avoid horror due to its intense or disturbing content, while others may steer clear of romantic roles because of personal boundaries. Additionally, certain genres may not resonate with your strengths or career objectives. Knowing clearly which genres or roles you choose to *avoid,* ensures you remain authentic and comfortable in the projects you say *"yes"* to.

17. Would you still feel fulfilled if you never got to do the genre of movies/TV you prefer?

You must consider this realistically, since acting opportunities rarely align perfectly with your preferences, especially early on. You might find yourself accepting roles outside your favorite genres to build experience, exposure, or financial stability. Reflect honestly on whether your passion for acting itself outweighs genre preferences. If your fulfillment relies heavily on working within a specific genre, you may face frustration. However, if you genuinely enjoy the craft and the process regardless of genre, you'll likely have greater resilience and satisfaction throughout your acting career.

18. Would you be happy if all you ever booked were short films, theater, or commercials?

Short films can offer creative freedom and meaningful storytelling experiences. The theater provides immediate audience connection and artistic fulfillment through live performance. Commercials can offer financial rewards and practical industry experience, even without widespread recognition. If your true satisfaction comes from the process of performing itself, regardless of scale or visibility, then embracing these less glamorous, but equally valuable acting paths can lead to genuine, lasting happiness in your career.

19. How do you define longevity in your acting career?

Longevity doesn't necessarily mean continuous fame or endless bookings. Instead, longevity could mean sustaining regular work in the industry, evolving artistically over decades, or maintaining financial stability through acting. Clarifying what career longevity looks like for you can guide your decisions, helping you build resilience, make realistic goals, and create a sustainable, fulfilling career path.

20. How do you plan to grow your resume/reel?

You need a clear strategy for continuously developing your professional materials, as your reel and resume directly impact your ability to book future work. Consider proactively seeking roles in student films, indie projects, local theater productions, or online web series to accumulate experience and quality footage. Collaborating with different filmmakers, directors, or peers on self-produced projects can also provide valuable material. Some actors even hire companies to produce scenes specifically for their reel. Regardless of your choice, regularly updating your materials and thoughtfully curating your reel to highlight your strongest performances helps casting directors, directors, agents, and managers quickly understand your range and potential, ultimately opening doors to bigger opportunities.

21. Which acting skills are you currently lacking or could improve on?

Continuous improvement is essential in this competitive industry. Perhaps you need deeper and stronger emotional depth, improved vocal projection, greater comfort with improvisation, or enhanced physicality in your live performances. Identifying specific skills you need to develop enables you to seek targeted training, classes, workshops, or coaching, ultimately making you a more confident, versatile, and successful actor.

22. How comfortable are you memorizing large amounts of text?

It's important to realistically evaluate your ability to memorize dialogue because actors are frequently required to absorb lengthy scripts, often under tight deadlines. Some projects, particularly productions related to theater, may demand memorizing extensive monologues or entire plays, whereas film or TV roles might involve rapidly learning and performing multiple pages of dialogue daily. Understanding your current memorization capabilities will help you determine if you need strategies or training to strengthen this critical skill. Improving your memorization methods can boost your confidence, ease performance anxiety, and make you more reliable and efficient as an actor.

23. How well do you take direction?

Directors may ask you to interpret a scene differently, adjust your emotions, or completely alter your delivery. Being receptive to direction without becoming defensive or discouraged will not only enhance your performance output, but also improve your professional reputation. Actors who can quickly process and apply direction become highly valued collaborators, increasing their chances of being rehired and recommended within the industry.

24. Are you comfortable with cold readings and auditions?

Actors frequently face situations where they're given minimal time to prepare, sometimes just minutes. Cold readings require you to quickly interpret a script, make character choices, and perform confidently under pressure. Honestly assessing your comfort level with this skill helps you identify whether you need to practice improvisation, script analysis, or adaptability in your acting. Strengthening your ability to handle auditions and cold readings confidently can significantly improve your audition performance and overall confidence as a performer.

25. Can you confidently perform in front of an audience or on camera?

It's common for new actors to feel self-conscious or a sense of nervousness. However, excessive anxiety and/or discomfort can significantly impact your performance, limiting your authenticity and emotional connection. Evaluating your current comfort level helps you identify if you need additional training, such as acting classes, workshops, or consistent practice. Doing so will develop your confidence, reduce anxiety, and ultimately lead you to delivering more compelling and believable performances.

26. Do you have a mentor to guide you on your journey?

A mentor can provide guidance, honest feedback, career advice, and industry connections that can help you grow and make informed decisions. If you don't have a mentor yet, consider seeking one by networking, taking classes, or building relationships with industry professionals. Learning from someone who has already walked the path you're on can help you avoid common pitfalls and accelerate your progress in the industry.

27. What do you think of different acting techniques/is there one that resonates with you more?

Acting techniques vary widely, each offering a different approach to character development and performance. Some actors connect with Stanislavski's system, which emphasizes emotional truth and deep character analysis. Others prefer Meisner's focus on instinct and reacting in the moment. Uta Hagen's technique encourages actors to draw from personal experience to create authentic performances, while Stella Adler emphasizes the use of imagination and the world of the character rather than personal memory. Some actors thrive with classical training, while others develop their own style by blending techniques. Understanding which method or unique adaptation works best for you can help refine your craft and strengthen your performances.

28. What advantages do you have?

Recognizing your unique strengths and abilities is just as important as identifying your weaknesses. Potential advantages could include a natural charisma, emotional depth, comedic timing, vocal clarity, a memorable appearance, a proficiency in accents/foreign languages, or even a relative within the business. Clearly acknowledging these strengths not only boosts your confidence but also helps you market yourself effectively to casting directors, agents, and managers, increasing your chances of standing out and booking roles.

29. Are you willing to continue learning and evolving as an actor?

Acting is an art form that requires ongoing growth, adaptability, and openness to new experiences. Industry trends, techniques, and standards constantly change, and successful actors never stop training or refining their skills. Being genuinely open to continued learning through acting classes, workshops, coaching, or simply seeking out challenging roles ensures your talent stays fresh and relevant. Actors who commit to lifelong improvement are often time the ones who maintain longevity, versatility, and professional fulfillment throughout their careers.

30. Do you understand that in the entertainment business, the odds are statistically against you?

The acting industry is highly competitive, and the reality is that most people who pursue it will not achieve long-term financial or professional success. That does not mean you cannot succeed, but it does mean you need to approach this career with a realistic mindset. Thousands of actors are working just as hard as you, with similar training and talent. Understanding that the odds are statistically low helps you prepare mentally and emotionally for the road ahead. Most professionals and coaches will not tell you this simple fact, but the statistical odds are not in your favor. If it were that easy, everyone would do it.

31. Do you recognize the importance of networking?

Recognizing the importance of networking in this industry is critical because, beyond your artistic talent/abilities, the relationships you build can often influence future career choices and opportunities. Networking is actively building/maintaining genuine relationships with casting directors, agents, managers, directors, fellow actors, and industry professionals. Opportunities frequently arise from referrals, recommendations, or connections you've cultivated over time. Understanding the value of networking and actively investing time in it can dramatically impact your career trajectory, leading to more auditions, bookings, mentorships, and professional growth opportunities, which you might not have been offered otherwise.

32. How many new networking connections do you plan to make each year?

Setting realistic networking goals allows you to actively track and measure your progress, helping to ensure consistent growth in your career. Whether it's attending events, workshops, classes, film festivals, or industry mixers, determine a specific number of new contacts you'd like to establish annually. Perhaps 5, 10, 20, or even 30, depending on your availability and comfort level. Regularly connecting with new industry professionals ensures you remain visible, informed, and engaged. This will ultimately increase your chances of being considered for future projects and career opportunities.

33. Do you have a strategy for improving your audition skills?

Perhaps your strategy is regularly attending audition workshops, working one-on-one with an acting coach, consistently practicing cold-reading techniques, or any other method of practice you can think of. Whatever it may be, creating a focused strategy ensures steady improvement, helping you approach auditions with greater confidence, consistency, and effectiveness. This will set you apart from many actors who do not seek consistent growth; just be very clear on the strategy you plan to create.

34. Do you have the ability to self-tape your auditions?

Self-taped auditions have become the industry standard, especially after the shift toward remote casting. Being able to record high-quality auditions from the comfort of your home, with clear video, good lighting, professional sound, and an appropriate background, can significantly increase your impact on the viewer. If you don't already have these skills or resources, developing them should become a priority. Investing in basic filming equipment, learning proper framing/lighting techniques, and becoming comfortable with auditions through self-taping will greatly enhance your ability to compete effectively in today's acting market.

35. Do you know where your local acting classes are and who their instructors are?

If you're serious about pursuing acting, finding the right training is essential. Do you already have a list of studios, workshops, or schools in your area? Are you familiar with the instructors, their teaching methods, and their reputations in the industry? Not all acting classes are created equal, and researching the best fit for your needs can make a huge difference in your growth. If you haven't looked into it yet, now is the time to start so you can train with professionals who will help you develop your craft and prepare you for the industry.

36. Can you emotionally handle the financial unpredictability that comes from the entertainment business?

Do you have the emotional resilience and practical strategies to handle the financial fluctuations this business brings, such as careful budgeting, creating a comprehensive savings plan, or maintaining alternative income sources? Understanding your comfort level with 'financial unpredictability' upfront can help you decide whether acting truly aligns with your lifestyle goals and financial expectations.

37. What does your current financial situation look like?

It's essential to assess this honestly, as your finances will greatly influence your ability to sustain yourself in this unpredictable industry. Do you have a savings account, a steady side job, or family support that can help you through lean times? Are you financially prepared for periods with little to no income coming in? Understanding your true financial resources and limitations upfront will allow you to create a more realistic and systemized budget plan that ensures you can sustain yourself comfortably as you pursue your acting goals.

38. How much money are you willing to invest a year into your actor training?

Being clear about this financial figure is important, because quality training, such as acting classes, coaching sessions, workshops, or headshots, is a critical part of building and sustaining your career. Properly investing in your craft can impact your skillset, confidence, and professional readiness. However, it's equally important to note that these costs should realistically balance with your budget and financial goals. Clarifying exactly how much you can comfortably allocate each year ensures that you consistently invest in your growth without causing unnecessary financial stress.

39. Would you reconsider acting if you knew it would not be profitable?

This simple question pushes you to truthfully and realistically evaluate your motivations and priorities. Acting often comes with financial uncertainty, and it's entirely possible that you'll invest more into your career than you earn back, especially early on. Honestly assessing whether your passion and love for the craft itself outweigh the need for profitability will help you determine if this career is truly sustainable for you. Being clear about your financial expectations upfront can prevent frustration and help you make informed/realistic choices about your acting journey.

40. Do you have any existing loans or debts?

If you have student loans, credit card debt, or other outstanding payments, how do you plan to manage them while pursuing acting? Will you rely on side jobs, careful budgeting, or other financial strategies to stay afloat? Pursuing acting, while under heavy financial strain, can produce stressful insecurities, which provide you less time to focus on your artistic practices.

41. Would you be willing to pursue another career while pursuing acting at the same time? *[Note: I am not talking about a temporary side job]*

This is an important consideration, as balancing acting with a parallel career can provide financial stability and reduce the stress associated with income uncertainty. However, managing dual careers requires discipline, strong time-management skills, and realistic expectations about your availability for auditions, rehearsals, and performances. Though this approach may not be ideal for everyone, it can sometimes offer the financial stability necessary for an actor's long-term success in the industry. Reflecting honestly on your ability to handle this balance helps ensure that you don't compromise your acting aspirations or your overall well-being, allowing you to build a sustainable and fulfilling career path.

42. What does the phrase "struggling actor" mean to you?

The term "struggling actor" gets thrown around a lot, but it can mean different things to different people. For some, it might refer to financial instability, juggling multiple side jobs just to afford rent. For others, it may mean long stretches without auditions, dealing with constant rejection, or feeling creatively unfulfilled. It is important to define what that term personally means to you, because your perception of "struggling actor" will shape how you view your journey and whether you are willing to continue when things get tough.

43. Have you calculated the financial costs of becoming an actor, and can you cover them?

Acting involves ongoing expenses, which are rarely ever considered. Just to live on your own will require payments such as rent, food, insurance, gas, electricity, and various amenities. On the artistic side, you'll need to be able to afford classes, coaching, headshots, self-taping equipment, travel (if necessary for auditions), membership fees (like union dues), and more. Carefully evaluating and budgeting these expenses upfront can help you avoid financial surprises later and set realistic expectations. Being clear about these costs from the start ensures that you're financially prepared, allows for smarter career planning, and ultimately positions you to sustainably manage the financial demands of this career path.

44. What is the current balance in your savings account?

Being aware of your financial cushion allows you to evaluate how long you can sustain yourself while pursuing acting, what lifestyle changes might be necessary, and whether you need a part-time job, a career profession, or additional income sources. A clear understanding of your financial situation empowers you to make accurate and informed choices about training, auditions, and career investments without putting yourself under unnecessary financial strain.

45. Have you created a step-by-step financial plan? What does it look like?

Your plan should include steady income sources, such as a main job, side job, or freelance work, while tracking a monthly budget that covers both living costs and acting-related expenses like classes, headshots, and auditions. Having at least three to six months of savings to cover expenses can provide a safety net during slow or exhausted periods. Additionally, setting limits on career-related investments, managing any existing debt, and establishing a realistic financial timeline for how long you can pursue acting before reassessing can help you avoid unnecessary stress. If you haven't created a structured financial plan yet, doing so will allow you to approach your acting career with greater stability and confidence.

46. How much money would you need to get paid to act in a poorly produced movie?

Everyone has a price, and while you may strive for quality roles, there may come a time when the paycheck outweighs the artistic merit of a project. Would you take the role for a few thousand dollars just to stay working, or would it take a much higher offer to justify attaching your name to something subpar? Some actors are willing to take lower-quality projects for financial security or exposure, while others set a firm price that makes it worth their time. Knowing your number helps you set boundaries while recognizing the realities of the industry.

47. What type of living situation is realistic for you while pursuing acting?

Will you need to live with roommates to cut costs, stay with family for financial support, or take on multiple side jobs to afford rent? Are you prepared for the possibility of moving frequently, living in smaller or less ideal accommodations, or sacrificing certain comforts to sustain your career? Understanding what living situation is feasible for you can help you plan realistically and avoid financial stress while pursuing acting.

48. What do you think of the entertainment industry in general?

Do you view it in a positive or negative light, or do you see both sides? I encourage you to use the blank space above to list five aspects you see positively and five you see negatively. This will give you a sense of what you know so far, as well as reveal other areas of knowledge you want to explore further.

49. Do you have a strategy to mitigate the potential stressors of rejection?

You may have said you can handle rejection, but if rejection is constantly present in an individual's acting career, without the right mindset, it can take a serious toll on one's confidence and motivation. The goal for you, should be learning to separate rejection from self-worth. Casting decisions are often based on factors beyond your control. Having a strategy to cope, whether it be a strong support system, meditation, or setting personal goals beyond just landing the role, can help you stay resilient. You must develop a thick skin, celebrate small wins, and maintain long-term perspectives. This will prevent rejection from derailing your passion and progress.

50. How do you handle competition and comparison in this highly competitive field?

The entertainment industry is filled with talented individuals, and it's easy to fall into the trap of comparing ourselves to others. However, focusing too much on competition can lead to self-doubt and frustration. Instead of comparing yourself to other actors' abilities, focus on improving your own skills, building your unique brand, and celebrating personal progress. Note your current progress in achieving this.

51. Do you behave appropriately under pressure?

Acting involves high expectations, whether it's performing live, handling last-minute script changes, or competing in auditions. Some actors excel under pressure, using it as motivation to deliver their best, while others become frantic and sometimes unfriendly. You've likely worked with a classmate in school whose personality turned harsh or uptight due to a high-pressure assignment. The same thing happens in the entertainment business; the difference is, a sour attitude here can cost you future opportunities. Before entering this field, ask yourself: how do you handle pressure, and can you truly put your best foot forward when tensions arise?

52. Can you separate your self-worth from the roles you do or do not book?

If you judge your value only by how often you get cast, it can be hard to stay confident and motivated when setbacks happen. A better approach is to see acting as a craft you are always working on, not a reflection of your personal worth. Focusing on growth, training, and a real passion for storytelling instead of external validation will help you stay resilient and self-assured, no matter how many roles you land.

53. Can you let go of a character after a performance?

As an actor, you will play a variety of characters, some with personalities, beliefs, or experiences vastly different from your own. Being able to step into a role without letting it affect your sense of self is crucial for keeping emotional balance. Some actors struggle to not bring their characters' emotions or mindsets into their personal lives, while others can easily shift between performance and reality. If you find it hard to separate yourself from a role, you may need to develop strategies like setting mental boundaries, debriefing after a performance, or practicing grounding techniques. Understanding how you process roles can help you keep a healthy balance between your work and your personal identity.

54. Do you expect overnight success, or do you have the patience to build your career over time?

Acting is rarely an immediate success story; it often takes years of training, auditions, networking, and minor roles before larger opportunities arise. If you're expecting fame or financial stability quickly, you may face frustration and disappointment. Patience, persistence, and a long-term mindset are essential for navigating the ups and downs of the industry. Too many people expect a big break within months of auditioning, but that simply doesn't happen for the majority of actors.

55. For you, how many years would you consider too long without booking a role before you start to rethink your plans?

Every actor has their own standards and limits. It's your job to discover what that is for you. Put a physical number to this question. Some of you may say two years, while others may say five or ten years. There is no wrong answer; just write down what is truthful to you.

56. How do you plan to protect your mental health in an industry that can be extremely harsh?

Having a strategy to maintain emotional well-being is crucial, whether it's through therapy, meditation, journaling, setting boundaries, or maintaining a strong support system of friends and family. Finding hobbies outside of acting and practicing self-care helps balance your emotional highs and lows. Developing resilience and knowing when to step back and recharge will allow you to navigate the industry without compromising your mental health.

57. Is your support system strong?

A strong support system, whether it's family, friends, mentors, or fellow actors, can offer encouragement, honest feedback, and stability during tough times. Acting can sometimes feel isolating, so surrounding yourself with people who believe in you can help you stay motivated and grounded. If you don't have a solid support system yet, it's important to start building one to ensure you have the emotional resilience needed for this career.

58. Are you more drawn to character-driven work or plot-driven narratives, and why?

Character-driven stories focus on internal journeys, emotional depth, and complex relationships, allowing actors to explore layered personalities and transformative arcs. These roles often offer more room for nuanced, intimate performances. On the other hand, plot-driven narratives prioritize external events, action, and pacing, which can be exciting and challenging in their own right, especially when working in genres like thriller, sci-fi, or adventure. Understanding which type of storytelling you connect with more can help you choose roles that resonate with your strengths and passions as an actor.

59. Are you willing to take on less-than-glamorous roles to gain experience?

In the early stages of an acting career, landing high-profile roles is not always guaranteed. Some actors settle for background work, student films, or low-budget projects just to gain experience. There is no right or wrong way to approach this; it's simply a matter of personal preference. While some actors choose to take this route, others prefer to wait for more lucrative projects. Regardless of the approach, it's important to discuss and decide on it with your representation beforehand; otherwise, you risk falling out of sync with each other.

60. What less-than-glamorous roles would you absolutely NOT take?

If you are not willing to take on any less-than-glamorous roles, which ones specifically? Are you open to doing background work, playing non-speaking parts, taking on cheesy commercial gigs, or acting in low-budget indie films? What about roles that involve physical comedy, extreme prosthetics, or unflattering portrayals? It's essential to recognize what you are not willing to do ahead of time.

61. Are you willing to have a business mindset to treat your acting career as an entrepreneurial venture?

Acting isn't just about talent; it's also about strategy. Successful actors treat their careers like a business. They recognize the importance of marketing, industry contacts, managing finances, and consistently pursuing new opportunities. To do this, you may be required to invest in actor training, maintain a strong online presence, build professional relationships within the industry, and actively seek your own auditions instead of always relying on your representation. Viewing the industry as a business rather than just an art form increases your chances of maintaining a long-term career in this competitive field.

62. How often do you keep up with industry news?

Staying informed about the entertainment industry is essential for any actor aiming to build a serious career. Tracking casting trends, major film and TV projects, industry changes, and key industry figures can give you a competitive edge. Consider the following entertainment news sources, such as Deadline, The Hollywood Reporter, Variety, and Backstage. Staying updated with industry news helps you make informed career choices, stay ahead of Hollywood trends, and position yourself strategically for future opportunities.

63. Are you aware of the roles played by other important figures in the entertainment industry?

Along with actors, you'll also work with directors, writers, producers, editors, and many others who put in effort behind the scenes to make a project happen. How familiar are you with their roles and how they operate? You don't need to be an expert in these areas, but having at least a basic understanding of how they work is a smart move. This knowledge will prepare you better for future industry interactions and help you make decisions on set that benefit not just yourself but everyone around you.

64. Do you have a healthy ego?

In acting, maintaining a balanced ego is essential. You need enough confidence to handle auditions, take risks, and put yourself out there, but not so much that you become difficult to work with or resistant to feedback. A healthy ego lets you believe in your talent while staying humble, open to learning, and adaptable in a collaborative setting. If your ego is too fragile, rejection and criticism can be overwhelming; if it's too inflated, it can push away casting directors, directors, and fellow actors. Finding the right balance keeps you confident yet grounded, making you a more professional and respected performer.

65. Are you considering drama school? Why or why not?

Drama school can be a valuable experience, offering structured training, industry connections, and a solid foundation in acting techniques. You'll develop skills in movement, voice, text analysis, and on-camera work, while also expanding your network of peers and mentors. Additionally, you can learn the skills needed to teach, opening up more career options. However, drama school can also be a significant financial burden. Many programs have high tuition costs, and actors often graduate with substantial debt and no guaranteed job prospects. Given the financial uncertainty of an acting career, taking on large student loans might lead to long-term financial hardship. Some actors opt for smaller workshops, private coaching, or on-the-job experience as more affordable alternatives. Carefully weighing the benefits of formal training against the potential debt costs is crucial when deciding if drama school is the right choice for you.

66. How do you plan to get an agent or manager?

Securing representation is a crucial step in an actor's career, but it doesn't happen overnight. Will you focus on building your resume with indie films, theater, student projects, or other experiences, or will you prioritize networking and industry events to make connections? A strong headshot, a well-crafted resume, and a professional demo reel give you the best chance when reaching out to agencies. When seeking representation, you can submit directly to agents, attend talent showcases, or seek referrals from acting coaches and fellow actors. Understanding the different approaches and having a clear strategy will increase your chances of finding the right representation to help advance your career.

67. How much time do you plan to dedicate to your acting each day?

Whether you're working on monologues, script analysis, voice training, self-taping, or spending hours on classes, the time you dedicate directly influences your growth. If you have a side job or other commitments, establishing a realistic daily or weekly schedule can help you stay focused on improving your skills and being ready for opportunities. The more disciplined and purposeful your approach to managing time, the more your craft will develop.

68. Do you understand the basics of text analysis?

Text analysis involves understanding a character's motivations, subtext, relationships, and the overall arc of a scene or story. It also includes recognizing beats, tone shifts, and the writer's intent. Without this skill, performances can feel superficial or disconnected from the story. If you haven't developed strong text analysis skills yet, investing your time in doing so can greatly enhance your ability to interpret and add depth to any role.

69. What type of roles do you see yourself playing?

Understanding your casting type and strengths as an actor helps you market yourself effectively and pursue roles that align with your skills and appearance. Do you see yourself as the leading man or woman, a character actor, a comedic presence, a villain, or a dramatic powerhouse? Are you drawn to emotionally intense roles, action-driven characters, romantic leads, or quirky, offbeat personalities? Identifying the types of roles that best suit you can help you target auditions, refine your branding, and build a reel that showcases your strongest performances. While versatility is valuable, having a clear sense of your natural casting range can make your career trajectory more focused and strategic.

70. Would you consider yourself to be more of a leading actor or a supporting actor?

Understanding your natural fit in the storytelling process helps you market yourself effectively and pursue roles that align with your strengths. Leading actors typically carry the story, requiring strong screen presence, charisma, and the ability to sustain audience engagement throughout a film, show, or play. Supporting actors, on the other hand, bring depth and dimension to the lead's journey, often playing best friends, mentors, and/or antagonists. While some actors naturally fit into one category, others transition between the two depending on the project. Identifying where you thrive can help you focus your audition strategy, tailor your reel, and approach your career with a clear sense of direction.

71. Which actors do you look up to?

Recognizing the performers who inspire you can shape your acting style, influence your career decisions, and support your artistic development. Do you admire versatile actors like Meryl Streep, Denzel Washington, or Cate Blanchett? Or are you more drawn to those with sharp comedic timing, such as Robin Williams or Melissa McCarthy? Perhaps you respect actors who have taken unconventional career paths, like Adam Driver or Florence Pugh. Identifying what attracts you to these actors—be it their work ethic, emotional range, versatility, or career journey—can help you clarify your personal goals and refine your craft.

72. Who are five actors you'd say you are similar to?

Identifying actors with a similar look, energy, or acting style helps you understand your casting type and where you fit in the industry. Are there actors who share your physical characteristics, comedic timing, dramatic intensity, or on-screen presence? Recognizing these similarities can guide you in targeting specific auditions, marketing yourself effectively, and setting realistic career goals based on where actors like you have achieved success. Agents and managers value when actors know who they resemble because it makes pitching their clients for roles easier. Having a clear sense of your "type" demonstrates professionalism, self-awareness, and a solid understanding of the business, which can make you more marketable and appealing to industry professionals. If you're unsure, seeking feedback from acting coaches, agents, or peers can offer valuable insights.

73. What are your five favorite movies and why?

Do you admire these movies for their powerful performances, their storytelling strategies, or their innovative filmmaking styles? Maybe you're inspired by character-driven dramas like *Forrest Gump* or *Good Will Hunting*, or captivated by high-energy action films like *Mad Max: Fury Road*. Whatever it may be, knowing your favorite films not only helps you define your creative influences, but it also gives you a way to connect on a personal level with various industry professionals, since agents, casting directors, and fellow actors often discuss movies as a shared language in the business.

74. What would be your passion project as an actor?

Every actor has a dream role or type of project that fuels their creativity and reminds them why they chose this career in the first place. Maybe you want to play a deeply emotional, character-driven drama, lead an action-packed superhero franchise, or be part of a groundbreaking independent film. You might also be interested in collaborating in areas outside of acting, like writing, directing, or producing. Identifying your passion project not only keeps you motivated, but it also helps shape your career choices by guiding you toward opportunities that match your goals.

75. Can you list 5-10 things more important to you than acting?

While acting may be a major passion, it's important to understand what else energizes your soul. For example, family, friendships, mental well-being, and meaningful relationships can all offer emotional support and stability. Many celebrities seem to have it all, but as we've seen before, not all are truly happy. Beyond acting, what are those 5-10 things you find more important that you will continue to nurture?

76. Does your religion or faith contradict your pursuit in acting?

This is an important question to consider, as the entertainment industry often presents situations that may challenge personal beliefs. Some actors find that their faith strengthens their career by providing moral guidance, resilience, and a sense of purpose, while others find the industry to be completely at odds with their values. Whether your faith goes against specific content, on-screen intimacy, or certain biblical representations, it's essential to recognize your boundaries and determine how to navigate them. Being clear about where you stand on this issue allows you to make career decisions that align with both your faith and artistic ambitions, without feeling conflicted.

77. How comfortable are you with sex scenes?

This is an important question to consider, as many film and TV roles include intimate scenes, and your comfort level should influence the roles you pursue. Some actors are fully open to performing sex scenes/actions as long as they are handled professionally with intimacy coordinators and clear boundaries, while others prefer to avoid them altogether, due to personal values, religious beliefs, or comfort levels. Knowing where you stand on this matter is extremely important, as it ensures you make career decisions that align with your comfort level and personal integrity.

78. How comfortable are you with nudity?

Nudity is sometimes required by the production in film, television, and/or theater, but whether or not you're comfortable with it is entirely personal. Some actors are willing to do full or partial nudity if it serves the story. Others prefer to avoid nudity altogether due to personal values, cultural beliefs, career considerations, or concerns about exploitation. It's important to remember that you DO NOT have to feel pressured into doing nude scenes to succeed in this industry. Many actors have built strong careers without ever doing them. Setting your comfort levels early and clearly communicating them to your agent and managers helps ensure you take on roles that match your boundaries and values, even if it means passing on certain opportunities.

79. Are there certain physical scenes or actions you would not partake in?

This could include sex scenes, nudity, extreme violence, stunts, or roles requiring significant physical transformation (such as drastic weight changes). Some actors are comfortable pushing these limits for the sake of the story, while others prefer to set firm boundaries based on personal values, comfort, or safety concerns. Knowing what you're unwilling to do ensures that you remain in control of your career and allows you the ability to confidently communicate your limits to agents, managers, directors, and production teams without feeling pressured into something that doesn't align with your standards.

80. Are there certain physical scenes or actions you would not do while in a relationship?

Being in a committed relationship while working or pursuing a career in the entertainment industry can be difficult, as intimate scenes, on-screen chemistry, and busy schedules can put pressure on couples. It's important to think ahead about whether there are specific scenes (such as kissing, nudity, or sex scenes) that you wouldn't feel comfortable doing once you have a partner. Some actors set clear boundaries out of respect for their relationship, while others keep a strong separation between their professional and personal lives. Having open conversations with both your partner and yourself about your comfort levels helps ensure that you make career choices that match your personal values and professional goals.

81. Do you see acting as having a more positive, negative, or neutral effect on your partner?

Based on your current relationship and/or past relationships, has acting had a more positive, negative, or neutral effect on your relationships? Acting comes with unique demands, which can cause strain on any relationship. The unpredictable schedules, financial uncertainty, and intimate scenes can all be very uncomfortable for your partner. How these factors impact your relationship depends on individual dynamics, communication, and personal boundaries. Some partners may view these challenges as part of the job, while others may find them difficult to navigate. Reflecting on your past experiences, how have your career choices influenced the stability, trust, or overall dynamic of your relationships? Understanding this can help you assess how acting fits into your personal life and what adjustments, if any, may be necessary to maintain a healthy balance.

82. If any, what compromises would you be willing to make with your partner?

If your partner were uncomfortable with certain aspects of your acting career, such as intimate scenes, extended time away for filming, or financial instability, what changes, if any, would you be willing to make? Would you turn down roles that involve nudity or romantic scenes, limit travel, or prioritize financial stability over pursuing riskier projects? On the other hand, are there aspects of your career that you would not be willing to compromise, even if it caused tension in the relationship?

83. What are your current morals? What do you define as right and wrong in this business?

Your personal values shape the decisions you make in your acting career, from the roles you accept to how you conduct yourself in the industry. Do you have definitive boundaries regarding the types of content you are comfortable with, such as violence, nudity, or controversial subject matter? Are there certain industry behaviors, like dishonesty, substance abuse, or exploitation, that you refuse to tolerate? Defining your own morals early on will help set firm boundaries, ensuring that you do not let yourself or others get walked over in the pursuit of success.

84. Which actors do you disdain and why?

There may be actors whose work, behavior, or career choices you do not respect or disagree with, but ask yourself, *why*? Is it due to their lack of professionalism, poor treatment of colleagues, or off-screen controversies? Some gain a negative reputation for being difficult to work with, while others may take on roles that feel uninspired or driven purely by financial gain rather than artistic passion. By identifying the qualities you dislike in certain actors, you can help yourself define the kind of actor and professional you want to be, while staying away from the qualities you dislike.

85. Are you willing to say "no"?

In an industry where opportunities seem limited, it's easy to feel pressured into accepting every role, request, or offer that comes your way. However, knowing when to say "no" is essential for maintaining your personal boundaries, professional integrity, and long-term career happiness. Would you turn down a role that conflicts with your morals, a contract that undervalues your work, or a project that doesn't match your goals? If you lack the courage to say "no" and voice your opinions, then this industry might not be right for you. You need to recognize how much power you hold in being able to say "no," because your choices shape your career. Standing firm in your decisions ensures that you stay in control instead of letting desperation or external pressures dictate your path.

86. Describe your stress tolerance on a scale of 1-10?

The entertainment industry is a high-pressure field characterized by rejection, unpredictability, and demanding schedules. If you rate yourself on the lower end of the scale (1-4), you may struggle with the emotional toll of auditions, career instability, or industry pressures. A mid-range tolerance (5-7) suggests you can manage stress, but you may need coping strategies to maintain balance. A higher tolerance (8-10) means you likely handle setbacks, long hours, and pressure well, without allowing yourself to become overwhelmed. Understanding your stress tolerance can help you identify areas for improvement and develop strategies to build resilience in a challenging industry.

87. Can you handle potential scrutiny of your appearance and performance?

Acting is a profession where judgment is constant, whether from casting directors, audiences, critics, or even social media. Your looks, voice, body type, and acting choices may all be subject to criticism, sometimes in ways that feel personal or unfair. If you struggle with taking feedback or find yourself deeply affected by outside opinions, this industry can be especially challenging. It's important to develop resilience and learn to filter constructive criticism from unnecessary negativity. Understanding that scrutiny comes with the job will help you maintain confidence and focus on what truly matters, which is your growth and craft as an actor.

88. What are you giving up to pursue acting?

In any profession we choose, we often have to give up something to pursue it. That might be time, money, relationships, or whatever else you may think of. Pursuing acting is no different. There is no right or wrong answer, but for your life, think about what you might be giving up to pursue acting. Are you willing to let go of those things? Take some time to honestly consider what you are trading away to follow this path at this point in your life.

89. On a scale of 1-10, how happy do you believe you would feel to pursue acting?

If you rate yourself on the lower end (1-4), it may suggest that the uncertainties, sacrifices, and instability of the industry outweigh the potential joy acting could bring you. A mid-range rating (5-7) might indicate that while you enjoy performing, concerns about financial security, competition, or career unpredictability could affect your overall happiness. A higher rating (8-10) likely means that you find deep fulfillment in acting and are willing to endure the challenges that come with it. Understanding your expectations about happiness in this career can help you determine if pursuing acting long-term is truly the right path.

90. If you are under the age of 18, do you have a parent who will be with you every step of the way?

This industry has its share of good and bad people. Many young actors have shared very graphic stories about being exploited. It's important for your parent or guardian to be your steady source of support, guiding and protecting you from potential harm. While not everyone in this industry is malicious, having a parent with you at all times will offer you greater safety. Don't be alone with another adult; always have your parent or guardian there with you. If you don't have a responsible person who will be there for you, hold off on this business.

91. Are you willing to get an education while pursuing acting?

Balancing an education alongside acting can be challenging, but it is completely possible. It can provide stability and additional career opportunities. Some actors choose to study theater or film to refine their craft, while others pursue degrees in unrelated fields as a backup plan. Would you be open to enrolling in college, taking in-person or online courses, while auditioning and working in the industry? Understanding whether education fits into your long-term goals can help you decide if further learning will support your acting career or serve as a practical safety net.

92. List 5-10 things that would make you NOT want to become an actor.

Just as there are elements that have drawn you into the possibility of becoming an actor, there are equal counterpoints that would push you away from pursuing this path. What are those things for you? Be specific and detailed in your answer. By answering this question truthfully, you are further defining your boundaries on what you will and will not stand for.

93. If you had to quit on the idea of becoming an actor today, how much regret would you have on a scale of 1-10?

A lower rating (1-4) might suggest that acting is something you enjoy but could walk away from without feeling a deep sense of loss. A mid-range rating (5-7) could indicate that while you'd feel some regret, you might be open to exploring other career paths that offer stability or align better with your lifestyle. A higher rating (8-10) likely means that giving up on acting would leave a significant impact on you. Understanding your level of regret can help clarify how important acting truly is to you and whether it's worth continuing to pursue despite the challenges.

94. Who is in your inner circle?

Think about the ten closest people to you, the ones who have the largest influence. Are they high-achieving go-getters, or are they lazy and stagnant? The easiest way to judge this is to ask yourself what they have accomplished in the last week, last month, and last year. Do they spend more time talking about their dreams and wanting something great, or are they actively chasing their goals? It does not matter what their goal is. It does not have to be related to our career, but the energy and people we surround ourselves with do affect us. If you spend time with those who are lazy, you will typically become one of them. On the other hand, if you spend time with those who are making something of themselves, that energy and determination will rub off on you.

95. Are you self-disciplined?

Are you able to motivate yourself, or do you get easily distracted? Do you wake up with goals to accomplish and plans in mind, or do you need others to remind you to work and make progress? Though luck plays a big role in this business, those who are self-disciplined and self-motivated are much better prepared when luck happens; those who need constant reminders face a tough road ahead.

96. How will you navigate an industry that has a history of alcoholism and drug abuse?

It's well known that the entertainment industry has a history of alcoholism and drug abuse amongst its members. Since it's such a difficult industry to break into—less than one percent become household names—it's remarkable how many stories about these issues emerge. What personal boundaries do you have, and will your support system help keep you accountable? If longevity is your goal and your well-being matters to you, you need these boundaries in place before you even consider setting foot into this business.

97. How easily do you succumb to peer pressure on a scale of 1-10?

A lower rating (1-4) suggests that you are confident in your decisions and unlikely to be influenced by others, even in high-pressure situations. A mid-range rating (5-7) may indicate that while you generally stick to your beliefs, you might occasionally feel pressure to conform in certain social or professional settings. A higher rating (8-10) suggests that you may struggle with standing your ground, which could be challenging in an industry where external influences, social circles, and professional expectations can push actors beyond their comfort zones. Understanding where you fall on this scale can help you identify areas where you may need to strengthen your boundaries and decision-making skills to navigate the entertainment industry with confidence and a better sense of self.

98. If you achieved mainstream success, what would you do with that fame and money?

Those fortunate enough to become household names often earn substantial wealth and wield significant social influence. How you choose to use these benefits depends on your priorities. Would you focus on sustaining financial stability through investments, business ventures, or funding personal creative projects? With fame, would you use your platform for advocacy, philanthropy, industry change, or would you prioritize privacy? Some actors use their success to mentor others and create opportunities for underrepresented voices, while others focus on maintaining a comfortable lifestyle outside the industry. Knowing what you would do with success can help you stay focused and prepared if that moment ever becomes a reality.

99. Are you considerate of what you post on social media?

Having a large following can sometimes provide extra benefits in this business, but the quality of what you post could have a drastic impact on your career. Post something too polarizing and casting may have second thoughts. It's not always fair, but that's the business we're in. So, before you create your next post, I'd ask yourself, *are you okay with everyone seeing this?*

100. What will you do during dry spells when auditions are not coming in and/or no bookings have occurred?

You need to accept that auditions don't always come in. I've known actors who are lucky to have one or more auditions a week, but on the other hand, I've also seen actors who get only one audition a month. When union strikes happen, the whole industry seems to hit pause or move extremely slow. What are your plans during those times?

101. What legacy would you want to leave behind as an actor?

Acting is about more than just securing roles; it's also about the impact you leave behind, both on and off the screen. Do you want to be remembered for a groundbreaking performance that pushes artistic boundaries or accomplish something most can only dream of? Maybe your goal is to inspire others, help change industry standards, mentor the next generation of actors, or create deep/meaningful stories that leave a long and lasting impression. Knowing the kind of *legacy* you want to leave can help guide your career choices and ensure your work aligns with your long-term vision.

The Last 11 Thoughts

1. Congratulations

Congratulations, you've successfully reached the end of the 101 questions. Take a deep breath and give yourself a moment to recognize what you've just accomplished. I assure you, the work you've done within these pages is profound. You haven't just passively read a book; you've actively engaged in a rigorous process of self-examination specifically designed for the complex, demanding, and often confusing world of acting.

Completing these 101 questions is more than just a simple intellectual exercise; it's an act of courage and resilience. It involves you challenging assumptions, questioning deeply held desires, and honestly examining your strengths, weaknesses, fears, and ambitions. You've explored the engine room of your own motivations and stress-tested the foundation of your resilience. This is work that many young and aspiring artists, caught up in the intoxicating whirlwind of the dream, unfortunately overlook. You, however, chose to pause, reflect, and prepare. You decided to invest in the most critical asset you possess in this industry, or any industry for that matter... yourself.

Reflect on where you were when you first opened this book. Maybe you felt lost, driven by passion but lacking direction. Perhaps doubts and conflicting advice swirled in your mind, or the vastness of the industry felt overwhelming. Now, compare that feeling to where you are today. You might not have all the answers—life rarely provides such clear solutions—but you are certainly clearer about your path. You've mapped out key parts of your inner landscape. You've recognized potential obstacles and resources. You've started to define your personal sense of success, your core values, and your level of risk tolerance.

This process itself is a victory. In an industry often fueled by external validation, such as landing the callback, signing with an agent, or rave reviews, you have taken a crucial step forward, powered by internal motivations. You've done the unglamorous but essential work that supports any hope of lasting success and fulfillment in a creative career. So, before you move on to the next part of your journey, celebrate this achievement. You've shown up for yourself, and you've treated your aspiration with the seriousness it deserves. Congratulations.

2. Your Compass

Think of this book not as a final destination, but as a vital navigational tool—like a compass, sextant, or detailed map of your inner world. You'll refer to it repeatedly during your journey. The answers you write here aren't set in stone; they reflect your understanding, feelings, and goals at this moment. Remember, life is constantly changing.

Remember the Formula 1 driver. They don't just glance at the map once before their first race and then forget about it. Instead, they often revisit it, because conditions will change. The weather shifts, car parts malfunction, and other competitors may alter their strategies. The driver must be constantly adjusting based on new information and their ever-increasing experiences. Similarly, your growth as an artist and a person will follow a similar path of change. Your priorities will shift, shaped by successes, failures, unexpected life events, new ideas, and collaborations with other artists.

This book is designed to be a living document. Dedicate time—perhaps annually, after a significant career milestone or setback, or whenever you feel lost or uncertain. Reflect deeply on these questions. Review your past answers. How do they resonate today? What has changed, if anything? Which core truths still hold strong?

Perhaps you initially felt motivated by a strong desire for recognition, but after experiencing the collaborative joy of a small theatre company, you've concluded that community and the craft itself have become more important. Revisit the questions about success and motivation. Maybe you had a definition of your ideal role early on, but after working with a specific director, it opened your eyes to a genre you'd previously overlooked. Re-examine the questions about artistic taste and goals. Perhaps a financial setback prompts you to reconsider your risk tolerance or your need for a side income stream. The questions about finances and lifestyle become more relevant again.

Treat this book as a trusted advisor you can revisit for an honest check-in. It's a tool to help you monitor your growth, stay aligned with your changing values, and make conscious choices instead of drifting reactively. Your future self will thank you for keeping this dialogue open. The answers might evolve, but the importance of asking these questions remains the same.

3. Embracing Your Evolution

One of the most valuable insights from this book is that it's completely normal for your goals, dreams, and identity as an artist to evolve. Our culture often promotes unwavering, lifelong commitment to a single path, with stories of those who knew their destiny early and pursued it relentlessly. While inspiring, this can create pressure and shame for those whose journeys are less linear or whose passions shift. Let go of that pressure. The self-knowledge you've gained through these questions is not meant to lock you into a rigid plan but to empower you to make authentic choices. If in five years you find fulfillment in directing, writing, teaching, advocacy, or work outside the arts, that's not a betrayal of your earlier self; it's an evolution—proof that you're listening to your inner compass.

Change can be challenging and may cause various feelings of instability or loss of identity. Yet, resisting authentic inner changes often leads to greater dissatisfaction over time. Imagine a river: blocking its natural flow requires enormous effort and can cause stagnation or uncontrolled flooding. Allowing the river to follow its natural course, shaped by the landscape, is a more sustainable and fulfilling strategy. Stay curious and receptive. If you feel drawn toward a new path, pursue it with honesty and introspection, just like with these 101 questions. Acting might become part of a broader creative journey. It could help you uncover related passions or expand your idea of an "artistic life' beyond simply performing.

Remember this key idea: *this journey is about YOU*. Your happiness, fulfillment, and personal understanding of a meaningful life are what truly count. Changing your goals isn't quitting; it's adapting your path with better insights—gained from your experiences and growing self-awareness. See change not as a threat, but as an opportunity for continuous growth and alignment in your career.

4. For Those Who Concluded Acting Is Not For You

As you worked through these questions, you might have gained a different kind of clarity. Perhaps you've concluded that the financial stress, instability, constant rejection, and lifestyle of an actor don't align with what you want for yourself. Maybe you decided that choosing stability and protecting your well-being is more important to you right now than pursuing a risky career in acting. That's not giving up. That's making an informed decision about what's best for you at this point in your life.

Understand that this isn't a failure; it's a sign of self-awareness and responsible choices. Reaching this point has saved you years of struggle, financial stress, and emotional exhaustion. This book isn't meant to persuade you to pursue acting or to abandon it. Instead, it's designed to help you ask the right questions. That doesn't mean acting will never suit you, but perhaps now isn't the best time, and that is perfectly okay.

If someone aspires to be a surgeon but, after careful reflection, realizes that the demanding, high-pressure, long hours of a surgical career aren't suitable for them despite their fascination with the field, we wouldn't judge or criticize them. Instead, we would understand their perspective. These insights aren't failures; they are informed decisions guiding someone toward a more fitting path. Apply the same compassion and understanding when evaluating your own choices.

5. Deciding To Pursue Acting While Having A Full-Time Career

Instead of abandoning acting completely, some of you might think that juggling acting with a full-time or well-paying part-time job offers the best chances. This approach allows you to maintain a lifestyle closer to what you desire and reduces your financial uncertainties. Although challenging, it is a realistic option that requires dedication, whether you're aiming for that once-in-a-lifetime role or pursuing acting as a hobby. I've seen many lawyers, officers, teachers, architects, and others participate in community theater or audition for large projects on the side, proving it's very *feasible* to do both. Whatever career path you choose alongside acting, make sure to plan carefully before diving in.

Pursuing acting passionately alongside a stable and viable primary income source is not a compromise or second best. Instead, it's a strategic and rewarding choice. It enables you to engage with your art form from a place of security rather than desperation.

Consider the advantages:

1. **Reduced Financial Pressure:** When your rent, food, and basic needs are covered by a reliable income, the pressure on every single audition is dramatically reduced. You can approach acting opportunities with less anxiety and more freedom. You won't be tempted to take soul-crushing jobs just to pay the bills.

2. **Greater Selectivity:** You can afford to be more discerning about the projects you take on. You can choose roles and collaborations that genuinely excite you and align with your artistic values, rather than grabbing at anything that comes along.

3. **Acting for Love, Not Survival:** This model allows you to keep your relationship with acting rooted in passion and creative exploration. It prevents the potential burnout and cynicism that can arise when art becomes solely a means to an end.

4. **Balanced Life:** It allows you to cultivate other interests, relationships, and aspects of your identity outside of the often all-encompassing world of acting. This can lead to a richer, more well-rounded life experience, which, ironically, can often feed back into your acting, giving you more depth and perspective to draw upon.

5. **Luck Without Desperation:** If "luck strikes," a side project takes off, or an unexpected opportunity appears, then that's FANTASTIC! You're in a position to benefit from it. But your core well-being and stability are not dependent on that sudden change. You have established a stable, sustainable foundation.

This approach demands discipline, strong time management skills, and a clear grasp of your priorities. You must set aside dedicated time for acting pursuits amid your other responsibilities. However, for many, trading the possible highs and lows of a full-time acting career for a more stable life that still includes meaningful artistic engagement is a wise and sustainable choice. It's just another way to navigate this journey on your own terms, based on the self-knowledge you've gained here. This doesn't mean you have to keep your current full-time job if you book something significant. If luck comes your way and you can pursue acting as your full-time career, then you should take advantage of it. Remember, if this path were easy and straightforward, everyone would choose it. Don't let anyone tell you this approach is a lesser option; for many, it's the smarter and happier choice.

6. You're All In On Acting

On the other hand, some of you, after facing the challenges, realities, and possible setbacks outlined in these questions, may feel an even stronger fire inside. The obstacles you've discovered haven't deterred you; rather, they've reinforced your resolve. You might now feel confident that taking action is exactly the right path for you, and despite any challenges, you can sense the desire burning inside. These realistic views did not weaken your passion. Instead, they made it stronger, helping you become more confident and firm in what you believe.

If this describes you, the work you've done here is invaluable. You've grasped the tough questions actors face and answered them honestly for yourself. Many in this situation usually make acting and the arts their top priorities. They are willing to sacrifice numerous life opportunities and other jobs to dedicate themselves fully to their acting careers. I know many couch-surfing actors, and while they are very happy with their choices now, there isn't much balance in their lives. They are currently struggling actors. Again, if this is your path, you are more than entitled to it, and you are still ahead of many other struggling actors who haven't answered these crucial questions. However, I want you to understand that, over the long run, maintaining this approach can be very challenging, as I've seen many actors follow this particular path to a dead end. So, you might want to think about finding balance within this approach and making sure you continue to stay true to your morals and principles while you pursue this path.

7. Building Your Strategic Blueprint

Before reading this book, your plan might have been vague or nonexistent, lacking detail, strategy, and misalignment with your goals. Now, you are in a much stronger position. Your answers to these questions serve as the foundation for creating a personalized, strategic plan designed specifically for **YOU**. With this new understanding, how will you proceed to develop a plan that aligns with your goals? Reflect on these aspects:

1. **Training**: Your responses about your strengths, weaknesses, artistic goals, and financial situation will help guide your training choices. Think about whether intensive conservatory programs are affordable and practical, or if targeted workshops on skills like on-camera acting or improvisation are a better fit. Private coaching might also work, or a combination of these options. Your self-assessment answers will help you use your time and resources wisely.

2. **Marketing Materials**: You should now have a much clearer understanding of your "type" as an actor, including the unique qualities you bring to a role and the kinds of characters you connect with. Knowing these details will help you create more

effective marketing materials by choosing the right type of headshots, making the appropriate demo reel, and building an online presence that truly reflects who you are. It's about strategically showcasing your authentic self and the roles you are after.

3. **Seeking Representation:** You will be much more attractive to agents and managers because you understand your career goals, like stage versus screen work, preferred genres, and your long-term ambitions. This type of clarity helps you find representatives who are the best fit for you. You can now speak more confidently about what you offer and what you're looking for in a partnership.

4. **Acting Selection**: When opportunities present themselves, your core values, artistic preferences, and career aims act as filters. Does this project align with the artist you aspire to be? Does it bring you closer to your goals? Does it honor your boundaries? You will make decisions that foster a career aligned with your vision, avoiding a scattered approach to your energy.

5. **Financial Planning**: Addressing the questions about finances, lifestyle, and risk tolerance compels you to develop a sustainable financial plan. This may include budgeting, exploring flexible side-hustles, setting financial targets, or making informed debt decisions. Achieving financial stability lessens desperation and enables you to make better career decisions.

6. **Defining Success**: Most importantly, you have established a personalized idea of what real success looks like to you. These questions have helped you create your own North Star, enabling you to track progress on your terms and at your own

pace. You can celebrate milestones that are meaningful to *you* and remain grounded in your own benchmarks.

Without the self-awareness you've gained from this book, any plan would have been unstable, susceptible to shifting moods, external factors, and failure. Now, you have a solid foundation to create a strategy that more accurately represents your true self and increases your chances of personal success and fulfillment.

8. The Book I Wish We Had

While writing this book, I often thought about my peers. They were talented and passionate individuals whom I had the privilege to train alongside. I remembered our late-night talks filled with dreams, fears, shared struggles, and hopes. Over time, I saw many of them slowly drift away from acting. One after another, I watched them leave the path, overwhelmed by debt, disillusionment, or exhaustion from an industry they never fully understood.

I wondered if this book could have saved them the time, heartache, and financial struggles they faced. I believe the answer is *yes*. It might have provided clarity and vision early on, helping some pivot strategically to find sustainable ways to pursue acting without ever having to walk away completely. Others might have realized sooner that the struggles following their pursuit of an acting career weren't what they imagined. This realization would have eased their financial and emotional burdens. Think about how many struggling actors there really are. Too many young, kind, and aspiring artists face mountains of debt, work low-paying jobs for their art, or give up on their dreams altogether. These factors highlight the importance of a book like this.

I wish I had known all this from the beginning so I could have shared it with my peers. It would have given them a framework to navigate this challenging landscape before they got lost or gave up completely. I hope this book will serve as that missing map for years to come for everyone who reads it. To guide you and others on a path that's both ambitious and sustainable, built more on wisdom and self-awareness rather than hope alone.

9. Focus On What You Can Control

One of the most challenging yet liberating truths about an acting career is understanding the difference between what you can control and what you cannot. You cannot control casting decisions, movie popularity, fame, fortune, industry trends, or the unpredictable nature of *luck*. Obsessing over external outcomes beyond your control often leads to frustration, anxiety, and a feeling of helplessness. Building a career in this field becomes almost impossible if you fall into this trap, fixating on what you cannot control.

The key question then is, *what do you have control over*? You control your preparation, work ethic, commitment, how you interact with others, and how you view yourself. You possess the ability to respond to rejection constructively by learning from it instead of letting it define you. Your attitude and outlook are within your control. Moreover, you decide on the projects to pursue and the kind of artist you want to become. Thanks to the efforts you've put into this book, *you have the power to define what success and fulfillment mean to you.*

Remember, you can find numerous small victories across your career. Next time you work on a project, ask yourself: Were you prepared? Did you perform your best in the audition room? Did you manage a tough situation on set with poise? Did you make a choice that reflects your artistic values? Did you learn something new from a class or project? These are all victories that are within your control.

By focusing on what you can control, rather than what you cannot, you cultivate a deeper sense of purpose and mastery that doesn't rely on external results. It empowers you to navigate this journey with greater intention and inner peace, regardless of where the path leads.

10. LUCK

Luck plays a big role in the entertainment business. You could do everything right for the next ten years, get a good agent, prepare thoroughly for each audition, receive quality training, work harder than the actor next to you, and still, success won't be guaranteed. This industry is very subjective, and it's people-driven. One casting director might not see you as the right fit for a role, but another could look at you as the perfect actor. We have no control over what goes on in the minds of the casting directors.

The same principles apply to directors and producers: you cannot control the thoughts of others, nor can you control the politics that happen behind the scenes. Imagine this, you get the opportunity to audition for your dream role. You've done all the research, received private coaching for just this part, and you aced the audition. You believe you've given it your best, but little do you know, behind the scenes, the producer has decided to cast their niece for the project. Such circumstances are beyond your control, but these types of scenarios happen all the time. And if it's not a relative, then a friend, if not a friend, then a past colleague. Whatever the reason may be for you not getting cast, the answer is usually never revealed, regardless of the cause.

This all means that when you land a role, luck is often on your side. A suitable casting director sees you as the perfect fit, there are no political obstacles behind the scenes disrupting your casting, and your talent and skills are aligned with the role's requirements. Every actor you admire has experienced similar luck; otherwise, they wouldn't be where they are today. However, be cautious about receiving too much luck early on. While I genuinely wish you success, don't let too many early winnings get to your head. Excessive early momentum can lead actors to forget about the concept of luck, causing them to believe it's fate, that they are more special than others. Such thinking can hinder realistic and grounded decision-making.

I knew an actor who turned down a major role and a contract worth hundreds of thousands because he didn't want to be labeled as the 'Disney kid.' He had many small wins early in his career and thought they would just keep coming, so saying no to becoming the next Disney star was easy. This particular actor overlooked how fortunate he was to be in such a position. He believed something just as big, if not bigger, would come his way in the following months. I am here to tell you that years went by, and he never landed any significant bookings. He left behind status, industry connections, and hundreds of thousands of dollars, all because he thought this business was easy. He didn't realize how lucky an opportunity he truly had.

A wise actor should assess each opportunity carefully and act on it when it presents itself. However, it's crucial to keep your boundaries in mind at all times. While we all hope for luck, if taking an opportunity means compromising a boundary that is important to you, it's not worth it. Ultimately, you must be able to look yourself in the mirror and feel content with the person you see.

11. A Final Word Of Encouragement

This marks the start of your new journey. The effort you've put into this book has paved the way for the next chapter of your career. The arts are naturally challenging; this has always been true and likely always will be, but you've taken the necessary steps to clarify your goals, understand yourself better, and anticipate what's ahead.

Keep applying yourself and stay committed. Make each decision deliberate and focus only on actions that support your long-term ambitions. While developing strategies and working hard aren't always fun—they can be demanding, exhausting, and stressful—the rewards they bring will be something your future self will thank you for.

If you're just starting out as an actor, this book has given you a solid foundation, offering you more informed insights and realistic goals, putting you ahead of 95% of actors. You'll approach the industry with a different perspective compared to those who are detached or rely only on hope. As mentioned earlier, this book will act as a vital reference, aiding you in assessing your progress, refining your goals, and establishing professional boundaries. This resource is uniquely customized for each of you, based on your own answers.

The path ahead will surely bring surprises, challenges, and joys you can't yet imagine. Face them all with the same courage and honesty you've shown here. Remember, your idea of success is yours alone to define and redefine. Stay true to your inner compass, and don't hesitate to adjust your course as you learn and grow.

I'm truly glad to have been with you during this vital part of your journey. Whatever choices you've made or path lies ahead, I wish you all the best. May you move forward with clarity, courage, resilience, and a deep sense of staying true to who you are.

Your journey starts now. Go forward and chart your course.

Acknowledgments

This book feels like the result of many meaningful conversations, thoughtful observations, and shared experiences within the lively yet challenging world of acting. While the words are mine, the spirit behind them belongs to a broader community of artists, actors, and collegiate colleagues. My gratitude goes out deeply to everyone who influenced this work, both directly and indirectly.

To you, the reader, thank you for engaging in this process of inquiry. Your willingness to honestly explore the questions within these pages is what brings this book to life. My deepest hope is that it offers valuable clarity for your journey ahead.

To my family, whose love provides an unwavering foundation, thank you. The support I received was a constant source of strength. Your patience during long hours of writing and your steadfast belief in this work were gifts beyond measure.

Thank you to the educators and mentors whose insights have deepened my understanding of this craft over the years. And finally, thank you to the community of actors (students, colleagues, and peers). Witnessing your journeys, honesty, resilience, and shared truths has been profoundly instructive and deeply moving. It is in the spirit of helping others navigate those same complexities that this book is offered.

With sincere gratitude, thank you to you all.

About The Author

Christopher Strombeck is an acting professor, coach, and multidisciplinary artist with over a decade of experience in actor training and development. His work spans both stage and film, with a teaching career that includes private coaching, classroom instruction, and large-scale digital education reaching millions worldwide. He has studied acting, writing, and performance at institutions including CalArts, USC, and Juilliard, with additional training from Harvard and Stanford. Known for his emphasis on clarity, self-awareness, and long-term sustainability, Christopher blends conservatory rigor with real-world practicality to prepare actors for the creative and personal demands of the industry.

"To thine own self be true."

~ William Shakespeare (Hamlet)

"Knowing yourself is the beginning of all wisdom."

~ Aristotle

www.ingramcontent.com/pod-product-compliance
Lightning Source LLC
Chambersburg PA
CBHW071129090426
42736CB00012B/2071